MASTERING YOUR MONEY

2022 EDITION

DAWN GREENFIELD IRELAND

ARTISTIC ORIGINS

TESTIMONIALS

THIS BOOK gave me goosebumps because I could finally understand a budget plan and SEE it clearly! I am so grateful to Dawn Greenfield Ireland for having written an excellent book on managing money. I was amazed at all the categories in the TOC. After reading MYM 2022 Edition, I give it a score of 100% EXCELLENT! Dawn covered areas that I would not have thought about. She is articulate and thorough, which is how she explained every section in MYM. I ended up being so excited to start my budget path from the clear instructions in her book. – M. Hightower

~

NO ONE really prepares us in life for the ins and outs of monthly budgeting and personal money management. Dawn Greenfield Ireland has filled that gap with these easy, confidence-building instructions! While reading Mastering Your Money, it occurred to me that it could help to prepare students, newlyweds, and young military personnel for success. The instructions are clear, concise, and easy to follow. It would be the ideal gift for anyone just starting out on their own, or for anyone needing to get their monthly finances organized and under control. Mastering Your Money 2022 Edition is destined to become the "go to" instructional resource on the subject. Every library and book store should have this remarkable little gem on their shelves. – Jeff Gonyea

THE REVISED edition of *Mastering Your Money* is just right to help us through these tough economic times. Budgeting has become a necessity for most people especially with rising inflation, a tight labor market, and a crippled supply chain. The links provided for realistic and useable budgeting guidelines are just what are needed both for today and tomorrow. You can't go wrong with this book. – Jacob Schulzinger

THE MASTERING Your Money 2022 Edition is a great resource and a damn fine piece of writing, as always. The best feature is the part on managing your check register. I never knew what that checkmark was for, but you made the explanation clear that it's for checks that have been processed. Seriously, my parents didn't even teach me that and I certainly didn't learn it in school. The layout and the examples provided are clear and easy to read and understand. And the length is appealing as well. This could be read in one or two sittings. – Joseph Lawrence Thompson

CONTENTS

Books by

Dawn Greenfield Ireland

Nonfiction

The Puppy Baby Book

Puppy Adoption and Beyond

What's Breaking Your Budget

Writers Preparation Handbook

Mastering Your Money

Online Classes

Writers Preparation Handbook

How to Format Word Docs Like A Pro

Fiction

The Alcott Family Adventures

- Hot Chocolate
- Bitter Chocolate
- Spicy Chocolate
- Boxed Set

Katz' Cat

The Thol Series

- Prophecy of Thol
- Gifts from Thol
- Love of Thol
- King of Thol
-

Science Fiction & Dystopian

The Last Dog

Texmexzona (TMZ)
Book 2 in the Last Dog Series

Forced Dreams

Coming Soon

Bill Hill's Pills
Book 2 in Katz' Cat Series

Books by my Alter Ego: DG Ireland

Bonded (#1) ~ Tothars (#2) ~ Tilted (#3) ~ Unforeseen (#4)

Mastering Your Money 2022 Edition by Dawn Greenfield Ireland

Published by Artistic Origins

Book cover for 2022 Edition by Brandon C. White /VictoryLaurel

Interior layout by Yours Truly (me)

ISBN:

- 9781940385440 eBook
- 9781940385457 Paperback

Multiple licenses are available for a corporate, educational, or training environment. Contact the author for details.

Dawn Greenfield Ireland

Artistic Origins

www.dawngreenfieldireland.com

Publisher's Note:

This book may contain references to specific commercial products, process or service by trade name, trademark, manufacturer, or otherwise, specific brand-name products and/or trade names of products, which are trademarks or registered trademarks and/or trade names, and these are property of their respective owners. Dawn Greenfield Ireland, or her associates, have no association with any specific commercial products, process, or service by trade name, trademark, manufacturer, or otherwise, specific brand-name products and/or trade names of products.

Please visit my website: http://dawngreenfieldireland.com/ and sign up for my newsletter and get the latest news before the public.

Created with Vellum

MASTERING YOUR MONEY

2022 EDITION by Dawn Greenfield Ireland

ACKNOWLEDGMENTS

Proofreaders find things by latching their laser eyes onto the page. I am so grateful for Jeff Gonyea—he has whacked me to no end.

My pal Joe Thompson provided insight that opened my eyes to the youth of today. Thanks, Joe!

Thanks to Monica Hightower for expanding the budget category table! How I overlooked these things is beyond my frozen brain.

Many thanks to my niece Rene Karolinski for all the research she did to make this book the best it could be.

Thank you Jake Schulzinger for once again reviewing this growing book.

Actions Appreciated

Please leave a review at your favorite retailer! Reviews help authors get recognized, get the word out and sell more books. I will love you forever if you leave a review!

If you would like to join my **postcard brigade**, I'll mail you 4 postcards. One for you and three to hand out. Email me your address and I'll mail them. USA only. All others, I can email you the postcard for sharing with your world.

Discounts & License Agreements

I provide corporate and educational licensing agreements and discounts for this book. Your logo can be placed on the cover.

SYMBOLS

The following symbols are used throughout this book:

	This is a note box. It contains information the author wants you to pay particular attention to.
	This is a hint box. It contains an enlightening, mind-expanding hint to save you from yourself.

ABBREVIATIONS/ACRONYMS USED IN THIS DOCUMENT

ACH	Automated Clearing House
ATM	Automated teller machine
CPA	Certified Public Accountant
EFT	Electronic funds transfer
Gen X	Americans born between the mid-1960s and the early-1980s, between baby boomers and millennials
IRS	Internal Revenue Service
NACH	National Automated Clearing House
NSF	Non-sufficient funds
PDF	Portable Document Format

1

INTRODUCTION

If you or someone you know is constantly coming up short of money in their checking account, or if you have transactions bouncing like basketballs, you have come to the right place.

No one ever taught us how to conduct personal business in high school, college, or even at home. When we were young and lived at home, we saw our parents living their lives, but we didn't know how they paid for things, where the money came from or where it went. Rarely do we grow up knowing what the cost of living means and how it affects every aspect of our lives.

We had a roof over our heads, food, clothes, and the necessities of life. Someone in the household went to work, earned money, and provided for us. Our parents dragged us to the grocery store, and the money was mysteriously there to purchase food. Same with either riding on the bus or in a car—a bus ticket got you a seat and money paid for gas in the car and off you went.

We go to high school, graduate, either get a job or go off to college and come out with a degree, but we have no practical life experience. Most of us start off with debt from student loans, car payments, and car insurance—responsibilities that may not have very much meaning because of our personal financial ignorance.

Sound familiar?

I was lucky. Years ago—actually decades ago—a coworker's wife, who was a CPA, sat me down and explained the mysteries of how to operate and manage a checkbook register so efficiently that I could track every dime I earned—literally.

It was easy!

It took very little effort, made sense and changed the way I looked at and valued money. Then, two jobs later, a coworker and her husband were going through a pretty tough time. They spent at least one week's paycheck a month paying insufficient funds charges while screaming and blaming each other.

I sat down with my coworker and showed her my system. Then she said the magic words:

You know what, Dawn? You should write this down.

Well, duh... I was a technical writer. The rest is history. The original *Mastering Your Money* won the New England Book Festival competition in the ebook category in December 2008.

How This Tiny Book Will Help You

Mastering Your Money will take the mystery out of maintaining your checking account. You will learn:

- How to create a budget.
- Why checks bounce (Hint: you contribute to this).
- What happens when a check bounces?
- How to make your checkbook register your financial guru.
- And how to maintain your checkbook so you can safely use online banking without disasters.

This book is perfect for:

- Young people getting started on their own.
- High school and college students.
- People starting over.
- Anyone thrust into the role of responsibility for their household.

2

BANKING STATISTICS & FACTS YOU NEVER KNEW

You cannot afford to be ignorant regarding money matters. The banking industry rules what happens in your checking account regarding fees and charges for transactions.

While people still write millions of checks each year, checks account only for about 12% of all non-cash payments, according to the *Federal Reserve*. It wouldn't be surprising if you rarely wrote checks—or never at all if you're younger than 25.

Millennials are **writing checks just about** as often as Gen Xers, with 59% of both age groups reporting that they've written a check within the last six months. Speaking of checking accounts, nearly 46% of respondents write one to two checks per month. (*Source: https://financebuzz.com/how-we-pay-survey.*)

In Europe and other industrialized parts of the world, electronic payment mechanisms have largely replaced checks. But in the U.S., **paper checks are still very common**, accounting for over 60% of retail payments. https://www.theverge.com/ad/16774328/american-checks-currency

https://www.gfmag.com/global-data/economic-data/hquidd-payment-instruments-checks

Personal checks can be useful because **some transactions still require checks**. Landlords may insist that tenants pay rent with checks, and some small businesses don't accept credit or debit cards.

The number of core non-cash payments, comprising debit card, credit card, automated clearinghouse (ACH), and check payments, reached 174.2 billion in 2018, an increase of 30.6 billion from 2015. The value of these payments totaled $97.04 trillion in 2018, an increase of $10.25 trillion from 2015. (*Source: The 2019 Federal Reserve Payments Study*, 2018.)

The number of overdraft transactions in 2020 fell to less than 1 billion after topping that mark for about two decades. When I originally published Mastering Your Money, statistics from 2003 showed the number of bounced checks was about 200 million, for a value of about $151.2 billion.

According to the National Automated Clearing House (NACH) data, of the 86.4-million transactions initiated in July, 2021, 33.23%, or 28.7 million transactions, failed, while 57.7 million were successful. https://www.business-standard.com/article/economy-policy/auto-debit-bounces-dip-in-july-indicating-bounce-back-in-economy-121081701226_1.html

The average non-sufficient funds (NSF) or bounced-check fee charged by a bank or credit union is $35.00. (*Source:* bankrate.-com/glossary/n/non-sufficient-funds-nsf 2021.)

What exactly is ACH and why it's important to understand

ACH is a technology that was developed by the Federal Reserve and is typically used for small recurring payments between consumers and businesses, such as payroll deposits or mortgage deductions.

There are two types of ACH transactions: credit and debit.

Because the ACH Network is based on the assumption of good funds and correct information between both parties, a bank transfer can fail for a number of reasons even after the transfer has been processed (examples include insufficient funds, payment dispute, closed bank account, etc.).

ACH returns can be referred to as "ACH disputes" or "ACH chargebacks" but while those terms might seem like synonyms, they are crucially different.

"Disputes" and "chargebacks" are terms used heavily in the credit card space and imply that there is a third-party arbiter looking at evidence to determine a fair outcome. That does not happen during the ACH return process. (*Source: https://www.dwolla.com/updates/how-ach-payments-work/.*)

With nearly 70 ACH return codes, an ACH transaction is not "disputed" nor is it "charged back" it is simply returned.

Check with your bank and find out what fees apply when a transaction is returned, unpaid.

3

YOUR BUDGET

Everyone needs one, and no one has one. A budget is critical to your financial well-being. This is where you examine money coming in and money going out every month and making sure there are no shortages.

Budget Categories

All budgets are not created equal. Your budget may differ considerably from a friend or relative's budget. If you own or live in a house, you may have expenses such as lawn care, and maybe pool upkeep that people living in an apartment wouldn't have.

Look over this list of categories for common expenses, and add specific categories to your budget to capture **all** of your expenses.

Common Expenses		
Rent, Mortgage	Medical / Life Insurance	Homeowners Association Dues, Renters / Homeowners Insurance, Property Taxes
Utilities: Electric, Gas, Water, Trash, Recycling	Lawn/Pool Services, Pest Control, Gardening, Snow Plowing	Transportation: Car Payment, Uber/Lyft, Bus
Prepared (ready-made) Food, Delivery Services	Eating Out: Breakfast, Lunch, Dinner, Snacks on the go, Coffee (Starbucks)	Pet Supplies, Vet, Boarding
Medical Expenses, RX, Therapy, Supplements	Savings Account, 401K, Investments	Gasoline, Auto Maintenance, Tires, Toll Road Fees, Annual Registration, Insurance, Inspection
Subscriptions: Newspapers, Magazines, Newsletters	Furniture	Housekeeper, Maid
Child Care, Child Support	Student Loans, Credit Cards	Gym / Spa Memberships
Personal Care: Haircut / Barber, Massages, ManiPedi, Facials, Tattoos	Shopping: Clothes, Shoes, Kitchen Gadgets, Makeup	Cellphone/Smart Phone, Smart Watch, Wireless Phone, Tablet
Internet, Premium Cable, Wireless, Streaming, Apps	Lottery Tickets, Betting / Gambling Debts, Pay-day Loans	Electronic Gadgets, TV, Computer, eBook Reader
Entertainment: Books, Movies, Music, Sports Events, Dog/Car/Horse Races, Hobbies	Small Business Expenses, Office Supplies	Tools, Lawn Equipment, Car Gadgets
Alimony, Back Taxes	Donations, Tithing to Church	Floral Arrangements, Gifts

Sample Budget

Study the sample budget to understand how this will help you build your own budget.

The monthly income shown in the sample budget is based on $38.45 per hour, or 160 hours per month.

> ☞ A blank budget is in the back of this book. You can also download a blank budget from: https://www.dawngreenfieldireland.com/living-smart

Payment Method*	Who Pays?**	Monthly Expense/Bill	Due Date	Amount $***
CK	Me	Rent (2-Bedroom apartment)	1	1,964
OL	Me	Electric: Summer / Winter	2	250 / 100
OL	Me	Gas (heat/cooking): Summer / Winter	3	30 / 159
OL	Me	Car Payment	3	563
D	Me	Transportation (Uber/Lyft)	--	80
Auto	Creditor	Cellphone	3	127
Auto	Creditor	Credit Card+	4	Bal
OL	Me	Car Insurance	15	140
Auto	Creditor	Internet	18	57
Auto	Creditor	Renters Insurance	24	37
OL	Me	Water / Trash / Recycle	27	71.41
D	Me	Groceries		387
D	Me	Gasoline		164
D	Me	Eating out		250
D	Me	Food Delivery		242
D	Me	HBO, Netflix, Disney+, DC Universe		40
D	Me	Child Care ($248 per week)		992
		TOTAL per month		$5214

*CK – check, Auto – automatic deduction, D – debit card, CC – credit card, OL – online bill pay, CA – cash.

** Me (I pay), Creditor pays

*** Rounded up to the next dollar

+ Credit card payment in full could eat a good portion of left-over money

Monthly Income: $ 6,152†

Budget: $ 5,214

Left over: $ 938

† based on $38.45/hr.

4

NATIONAL AVERAGES

When you create your budget you might wonder if your category amounts are high or low. The following links will provide information for you to compare your budget category amount to that of other people across the nation.

> Some of these websites may use popups. Do not click on any popups unless they suggest relevant content for your budget.

Average Household Budget & Expenses

- Average Household Budget and Expenses in America 2021 - Elite Personal Finance https://www.elitepersonalfinance.com/average-household-budget/

Apartment Rentals

- Apartment rentals by state, and national: Rent Report, October 2021: The State of the Rental Market https://www.apartmentguide.com/blog/apartment-guide-annual-rent-report/
- Zumper National Rent Report: https://www.zumper.com/blog/rental-price-data/

Mortgage/Housing

- What Is the Average Monthly Mortgage Payment? https://www.thebalance.com/average-monthly-mortgage-payment.
- Housing Market Predictions 2021 & 2022: Crash or Boom Next? https://www.noradarealestate.com/blog/housing-market-predictions/
- Average House Price by State in 2021. https://www.fool.com/the-ascent/research/average-house-price-state/

Utilities: Electric, Natural Gas, Water, Trash & Recycling

- Electricity Rates by State (October 2021) https://www.chooseenergy.com/electricity-rates-by-state/
- https://www.electricrate.com/data-center/average-energy-bills/
- Utility Bills 101: Average Cost of Utilities https://www.move.org/utility-bills-101/
- What's The Average Cost Of Utilities? 2021 (movebuddha.com)

- Water Prices By State 2021 (worldpopulationreview.com)
- Average Utilities Cost in 2021 – A Complete Overview https://balancingeverything.com/average-utilities-cost
- 2021 Cost of Junk Removal | Debris, Waste & Trash Pickup - HomeAdvisor https://www.homeadvisor.com/cost/cleaning-services/remove-waste/

Transportation/Food Delivery

- The U.S. Rideshare Industry: Uber vs. Lyft - Bloomberg Second Measure https://secondmeasure.com/datapoints/rideshare-industry-overview/
- **https://backlinko.com/uber-users**
- 2021 Food Delivery Service Statistics You Need to Know | Beambox https://beambox.com/townsquare/food-delivery-service-statistics

One-third of online orderers will pay more than $50 for their meal.

Average Car Payment

- https://www.lendingtree.com/auto/debt-statistics/

Child Care

- Average Cost of Child Care by State https://www.move.org/child-care-cost/
- This is how much child care costs in 2021 https://

www.care.com/c/how-much-does-child-care-cost
- What is the average cost of daycare? https://www.carelulu.com/daycare-cost

Streaming Apps

- Average Consumer Spends $273 Per Month on All Subscription Services https://tvline.com/2021/09/29/how-much-people-spend-on-netflix-hulu-other-subscription-services/

Cellphone & Internet

- How Much Americans Spend on Internet, Streaming, and Cell Phone Bills https://www.reviews.org/internet-service/cost-of-internet-streaming-and-cell-phone-bills/
- How to save money on your phone bill
- https://www.cnbc.com/2021/06/15/how-to-save-money-on-your-phone-bill
- Average cellphone plan cost is $113 | Cost factors https://www.allconnect.com/blog/average-cost-of-cellphone-plan

Eating Out

- The True Cost Of Eating Out (And How To Save) https://www.moneyunder30.com/the-true-cost-of-eating-in-restaurants-and-how-to-save
- Consumer Expenditures - 2020 https://www.bls.gov/news.release/pdf/cesan.pdf
- Average Household Budget and Expenses in America

2021 https://www.elitepersonalfinance.com/average-household-budget/

Average Cost of Groceries Per Month

- https://www.gobankingrates.com/saving-money/food/average-cost-of-groceries/

Credit Card Payment

- 2021 Credit Card Debt Statistics https://www.lendingtree.com/credit-cards/credit-card-debt-statistics/
- How Much Is the Average Monthly Credit Card Bill? https://wallethub.com/answers/cc/average-monthly-credit-card-bill

Medical Expenses: Health Insurance, Hospital & Surgery, RX & Supplements

- What is the Average Cost of Health Insurance? 2021 https://quotewizard.com/health-insurance/how-much-does-health-insurance-cost
- How Much Does Individual Health Insurance Cost? https://www.ehealthinsurance.com/resources/individual-and-family/how-much-does-individual-health-insurance-cost
- Hospital and Surgery Costs – Paying for Medical Treatment https://www.debt.org/medical/hospital-surgery-costs/

- The US Prescription Drug Report 2021 https://www.nicerx.com/prescription-drug-report-2021/
- 18 Supplement Industry Statistics To Watch Out For in 2020 (moderngentlemen.net)

Newspaper Subscriptions

- Newspaper Subscriptions Cost in 2021. https://www.thepricer.org/newspaper-subscriptions-cost/

5

DOUBLE PAYMENT, NO PAYMENT, LATE PAYMENT

It's important to keep track of who pays what. When you have automatic payments, you may forget that you set this up with the creditor and accidentally add it to your online bill pay. This means you will have a double payment. If you are on a strict budget, those two transactions for the same bill may cause transactions to bounce in your bank account.

Likewise, if you manually pay your bills with either a check, or with online bill pay at your bank and forget to pay the bill, your creditor will ding you for nonpayment or a late payment, and they may charge you fees.

Also, keep in mind that when you write a check, you have to stick it in an envelope and slap a stamp on the envelope. Then you have to mail it. If you forget to mail the envelope, it won't get delivered on time, which will make your payment late.

Study the sample budget. You will notice the first two columns: Payment Method and Who Pays.

Payment Method

There are many ways to pay your bills and expenses: by check, automatic deduction, debit card, credit card, online bill pay through your bank, and cash.

An automatic deduction could be from either the creditor's website, or your bank through online bill pay. It is important to note on the budget in the payment method column, where each of these transactions is processed to avoid double deductions.

Who Pays?

This is the second most important column to pay attention to. This is where you note who pays the bill. **Me** means you pay the bill. This could be by writing a check, or visiting your online bank account bill pay function and paying the bill through your bank.

Creditor means you have set up automatic payment through the creditor's website. This could be for your cellphone payment, cable and/or internet, car payment, or any of your regular payments whether they are monthly, quarterly or annually.

You will notice for creditor payments, the Payment Method column shows Auto. This means that you have set up an automatic deduction transaction for a specific amount of money to be deducted on a specific day every month, or however the timeframe for this transaction is due (weekly, bi-weekly, monthly, quarterly, annually).

Reminders

It only takes a few minutes to set up bill payment reminders. Creditor and bank account websites should have a reminder for bill payments. To avoid late payments or missed payments, set up a reminder one or two days before the due date of your bill. That way you will not have late fees, or credit dings from forgetting the bill was due, and you missed the date.

6

GETTING STARTED

Income

Most income is direct deposited to your bank account through electronic funds transfer (EFT), and will appear on your bank statement. You can download your bank statements as a PDF, or other file types to your computer.

It would be beneficial to create a file on your computer with the year and name of the bank (if you have more than one bank account) to easily keep track of transactions. Example: 2021 Bank Statements – Broadway Bank.

Some companies pay with a company check and will provide either a manual or electronic pay stub. In this case, gather up any pay stubs or bank statements that show your deposits so you can determine your monthly income. If the job pays weekly, you should have four pay stubs. Bi-weekly is twice a month.

Income Sources

The following are common income sources:

- Pay check
- Alimony
- Child Support
- Trust Fund
- Social Security
- Disability
- Pension
- Small Business Income
- Restitution

Your budget should **never** depend on income that stems from overtime or an expected bonus. If your hours are reduced and your budget depends on overtime, you are already in trouble. If the company quarter, or year isn't as robust as expected, your bonus may evaporate or be greatly reduced.

> Treat overtime as a bonus. Add it to your savings account (or start one), or use it to pay down your debt.

Include child support, alimony, or anything else you receive every month **regularly**. Any income that comes in occasionally should be considered a bonus and **not** be included in your monthly income.

Get the calculator (you should have one on your phone or your computer) and add your monthly income. Jot down the amount. Remember, this is only **steady, reliable income**.

Next, collect all of your bills and arrange them in the order they are due. Have your checkbook handy to search for regular spending habits.

If you keep receipts for groceries, gasoline, and anything else you pay with cash, debit or credit cards, grab those as well, or refer to your bank statements or credit card statements for monthly amounts.

Now that you have your bills, checkbook, statements, and receipts in front of you, look at the sample budget.

Print out the blank budget, or grab a sheet of paper, or open a blank budget on your computer. List everything you pay out each month. Be sure to include food purchased at a grocery store, eating out/delivery, entertainment, gasoline, and anything else you **purchase** on a steady basis.

Gather bank and credit card statements, along with any monthly bills you receive in the mail, or those that are emailed directly to your inbox.

All repeated transactions should be in your budget.

After you have everything listed, start including the amount you spend on each line item. If you use your debit or credit card to pay for most items, it will be easy to identify and add up each line item's total.

If math isn't your best ability, use a calculator to be as accurate as possible.

Add up each line item or category to get the monthly amount spent in that category. Check off each item so you do not duplicate an amount in the final calculation. Enter those amounts on their specific lines in the **Amount** column as shown in the sample budget.

Next, after everything has a dollar amount in the category, add up all the dollar amounts in the Amounts column. This is your total budget amount.

Write the amount of your income on the **Monthly Income** line under your budget.

Write the amount of your budget under your monthly income figure. Subtract the budget from the monthly income. The amount left over can go into your savings account or pay down your debt.

Monthly Income:	$ 3,600
Budget:	$ 3,348
Left over:	$ 252

If the amount is a negative figure (your budget exceeds your income), stay calm. With everything laid out in front of you, determine which items can be reduced so you can meet your budget.

For example, if your entertainment expenses are exorbitant, highlight those items. You can tighten your belt and reduce the number for entertainment.

> It is far more important to pay your bills on time and have a good credit rating than to be entertained! If your lights are turned off or you do not have gas for the car, you should realize that sacrifice is called for. And... it won't be forever!

Examine your cellphone plan to determine if you are overpaying for what your typical usage is.

If you have separate companies for a landline telephone, cable TV, and Internet, explore an all-in-one plan that will loosen up your budget. I saved $70 per month when I chose that route.

Many people save a ton of money each year by bringing their lunch to work. You can buy a soft cooler for under ten bucks. Many come with the freeze packs included in the purchase.

Not only will you save money by not eating out, it is highly likely you will reduce your grocery bills by eating left-overs. You may also discover you have reduced the amount of food typically thrown out at the end of the week because (drum roll here) YOU ATE IT! And guess what? You just saved space in the landfill by consuming your food.

Another reason to make and bring your lunch to work is when you cook your own food from scratch, you won't be getting additives you can't pronounce, thereby eating healthier.

Everyone benefits when you tighten your budget.

7

GET ORGANIZED

Take this budget business one step further to expand your organizational awareness. Buy a file box and file folders. Use the entries on your budget or label the file folders January through December. Place your receipts and paid bills in the file folders.

Have you ever had to return something to a store and you couldn't find the receipt? You'll never have to worry about that anymore—the receipt will be in your file folder.

One weekend I went grocery shopping and bought a whole chicken for Sunday dinner. I was just getting ready to open the package when a rather pungent odor wafted from the package. I went to my file folder and grabbed the receipt, the stinky chicken, and exchanged it without a problem.

When you pay a utility bill, installment payment or other monthly account, write the date, manner of payment (check, paid with online banking, auto-deduction) and the amount on your portion of the receipt/statement.

If you have to speak with a customer service representative, make notes directly on your copy or portion of the receipt/statement. When you file it away, you have the record of the conversation in case someone promised something, and they did not follow through.

At the end of the year, you can throw out all the grocery receipts and utility bills that are not important. Keep any receipt for major purchases which constitutes a warranty in its own file, such as appliances, furniture, equipment. Consider using the calendar on your phone or computer to set up an alert for all your warranties.

For example, if your refrigerator begins to act up (making a noise, not cooling properly), and it is in the last month of the warranty period, get it checked out because after the warranty expires, even by one day, you are responsible for the bill. It only takes a minute to add the warranty expiration date to your calendar.

These easy practices will become good habits and you may discover you enjoy being organized.

Many years ago, the IRS audited me. Most people would quake in their boots. I grabbed my files and went to the appointment. Every time the agent asked for something, I pulled the receipt from my file box. I left there with them owing me fifty bucks instead of me having to write the check.

Now that you're familiar with a budget, let's move on to your checking account.

8

YOUR CHECKING ACCOUNT UP CLOSE AND PERSONAL

People Still Use Checks

Yes. There are still companies that would prefer a check over a debit/credit card.

https://investorjunkie.com/banking/are-personal-checks-still-necessary/

Safety First

When you are setting up a checking account and choosing new checks, do not include your driver's license, date of birth, or Social Security number on checks. Decades ago, those things were common on printed checks until someone with a brain snapped to the realization that with those things, a crook could have a field day at your expense.

Your identity is at stake and identity theft is the No. 1 threat today. No banking official would even suggest you adding those numbers on your new checks.

If you misplace your checkbook, forget it at the mall, or it drops out of your purse or pocket in a parking lot, the person who finds it may not be honest.

When someone has your driver's license number, date of birth, and Social Security number, they can apply for credit cards, store accounts, buy furniture, vehicles, even houses because you provided everything they need to get credit approved.

All a thief would have to do is create a fictional life with your credit report history that they got with your date of birth, which is conveniently on your driver's license, and Social Security number.

They may rent a post office box for your new life and just have a dandy of a time living high on the hog with your credit.

Routing and Account Numbers

It's a good thing to know the parts of a check. If you're just starting out opening your first checking account, you may not be familiar with how to even write a check.

This section of *Mastering Your Money* will identify the numbers and symbols on a check so you will understand them.

We live in an age of convenience, and there may be times when you may have to provide a routing number and your bank account number.

You may need routing and bank account numbers for:

- Direct deposit
- Online banking
- Paying online with an eCheck
- Paying bills with automatic deductions

Check Parts

The sample check may differ slightly from your check, but mostly, all the components identified on the sample should appear on your check.

1. Your Name and Address.
2. Check Number - Every check has a different number. It also appears at the bottom of the check by the routing and account numbers.
3. Date Line - Date you write the check.
4. Fraction - The bank's location and branch identification numbers.
5. Pay to the Order of - Where you write the name of the person or business you are paying.
6. Dollar Amount - Printed in numerals ($40.25).
7. Dollar Amount - Written (Forty and 25/00).
8. Security Mark - There may be an explanation on the back of the check for signature line, bank stamping, etc.
9. Memo Line - You can write yourself a note (replaced battery in car).
10. Signature Line - Where you sign your check.
11. Bank Logo and Address - Typically the main branch of the bank.
12. Bank Routing Number - The electronic address for your bank.

13. Checking Account Number - Where your money is located in the bank's electronic system.
14. Symbols - Weird little marks for the magnetic reader.

Sample Check

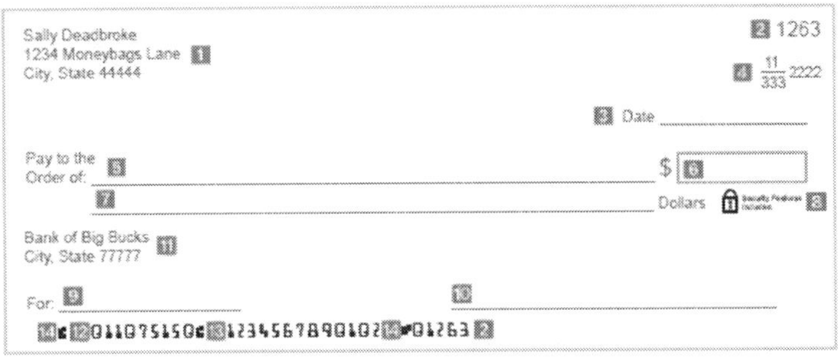

When you order checks, consider the type of checks that offer carbon copies that stay in your checkbook.

Why Me?

We live in an era of instant access. You can no longer depend on transactions taking several days to process through the banking system. It now happens at the click of a button when you use your debit card, or go to an automated teller machine (ATM) and make a transaction.

Cash flow, poor bookkeeping habits, a lack of understanding of the banking system, drastic change in salary—there are many reasons overdraft notices arrive from your banking institution.

In the 40 plus years that I have been using this system, only one check bounced, and that was because a grocery store clerk forged the amount on the check and added a one-hundred-dollar tip for herself.

Regardless of who's at fault, it is costly to overdraw your account. The bank may charge you $35 when you bounce a check.

The merchant may charge you an additional $20 to $40. This is for one non-sufficient funds (NSF) item.

If you miscalculated your checkbook balance and wrote several checks, those fees apply to every check that is over your balance.

Some banks also charge a **daily** fee for **every day** your account is overdrawn.

If your bank links your checking account to your savings account, there may be a fee for automatically transferring funds from one account to another.

Call your bank to get the facts and fees.

> Be sure to check with your bank regarding overdraft fees. Some banks charge an annual fee, others charge as much as $35 per check.

The terrible part is, if that bounced transaction was for a $5.41 purchase at the store, it could cost you $45 or more to clean up the problem.

If you know you do not have the funds to cover a check or transaction, do not write a check or make that transaction.

If a bank or merchant suspects you of **check kiting** or **paper hanging,** you may find yourself in serious trouble.

Check kiting is a fraudulent technique used to delay a check from bouncing and may involve multiple checking accounts.

Paper hanging is embezzlement where the paper hanger intends to pass a bad check to defraud either the bank or a business.

Depending upon which city, county, and state you live in, hot check offenses are punishable under either misdemeanor or felony charges, with fines ranging from $200 to $10,000.

They may also assess civil penalties.

You are also in jeopardy of receiving a sentence from six months to up to 20 years in prison. Check with your local office of the District Attorney for details.

Some grocery stores and retail businesses track customers who frequently get cash back from purchase transactions to observe patterns to detect illegal transactions.

With many service companies like TeleCheck, it is becoming more and more difficult for people who bounce checks to pay bills or to go shopping with a check or debit card.

These service companies are **reporting** companies.

Places such as banks, retail stores, apartment complexes and other businesses rely on the information provided by these service companies when deciding whether to grant or deny credit to you based on the information provided.

Not everyone has a built-in understanding of how to manage his or her money. Not everyone can cope with a checkbook.

My best friend used to wait six months before she tackled the bank statements, and by that time, disaster struck. (Luckily, her husband took over, and he coped very well.)

Forgotten Pitfalls

Money goes out of your checkbook in several ways:

- Bank service charge fee
- Check order fee
- Safe deposit box fee
- Automatic monthly deductions
- Automatic teller withdrawals (ATM/Banking Card, Debit Card, Pulse, etc.)
- Annual fees

These things aren't secrets; you just don't think about them, and that's dangerous.

Every penny adds up, and if you are on a tightrope budget, one forgotten transaction is all it takes to send that overdraft slip in the mail.

You thought you had enough money in the bank, for once, to see you through until the next paycheck.

Guess what?

Remember the new checks you ordered? They were sent to you, and the cost was deducted from your account, causing an avalanche.

The other day when you were rushing to lunch, you needed cash, so you stopped and used your bankcard in an ATM.

Bingo! That stops all other transactions, including **deposits**, and your account was zapped. Poor timing! Most debit transactions are processed as you complete your transaction at the cash register.

Look at your statement and find the statement date. That is approximately when the bank attaches the service charge to your account.

If you do not have a fee-free checking account or if you dip below the required balance, they will assess a fee.

> Fees and services vary among banks. Check with your bank to find out if your account will be assessed fees monthly, or only if your balance dips below a specified amount.

If you were not aware of this charge and you were low on cash at that point, a check, debit, or automatic bill pay transaction may be processed and bounced—sometimes by a mere few cents, if the funds are not there or if you do not have overdraft protection.

Paying with automatic deductions is great, but don't forget, every month that specific amount will be deducted from your account, and it doesn't always coincide with your pay periods.

This is more hazardous if you are paid twice a month.

For example, bi-monthly pay periods for months with five weeks make a long stretch between paychecks.

Just a day or two of waiting and praying for that paycheck to arrive to cover transactions can be disastrous.

Automatic deductions roll on.

9

HOW MUCH CASH DO YOU HAVE?

If it's been many months since you balanced your checkbook against your statements, you may be better off closing the account and starting from scratch.

You can't grab the cash and run; you have to wait one or two months for outstanding transactions to clear your bank.

In the meantime, you can open a new checking account and begin practicing good record keeping.

With the *Mastering Your Money* instructions, you CAN reconcile (balance) your checkbook no matter how long it has been. As long as you have bank statements, a box full of receipts, and your old checkbook registers, you can tackle the monster and tame it.

> If you misplace a statement, you can get a copy from your bank or go online and download the statement if you subscribe to online banking.

What You Will Need

- Calculator
- Ruler
- Pen or pencil
- Highlighter
- Whiteout
- Bank statements from current and previous months
- Checkbook registers
- Piece of paper
- Peace and quiet

Clear the calculator back to zero, send the kids to bed, put the dog outside or in the kennel, and cover the birdcage.

Make sure the TV is turned off, the stereo is turned down or off, and you have allotted enough time to be by yourself.

Take a Good Look

Don't panic!

If you do not have your bank statements, you typically can download them from the Internet if you signed up for online banking.

Download any statements you have not reconciled.

If you have several bank statements you never opened, now is the time. Open the bank statement envelope, remove the checks (if your bank provides them) and set the checks aside. Next, remove the statement and open it up.

The statement tells you the following, which are shown on the bank statement example:

1. The Statement Period
2. Items Enclosed*
3. Account Summary
4. Service Charge (Maintenance Fee)
5. Interest**
6. Deposits and Credits
7. Checks and Debits
8. Daily Balances
9. Closing Balance (Amount in the account at the time they charged you the service charge)
10. Automatic teller (ATM/Banking Card) transactions
11. Drafts
12. Fees (ATM withdrawal, maintenance fee)

----

* *If your bank does not return your checks in your statement, they may not list this line item on your statement. Your bank may provide copies of the check on the last page(s) of your statement.*

** *You will receive interest only if you opened an interest-bearing account.*

Sample Bank Statement

Bank of Big Bucks	Sally Notsorich 1010 Moneybags Lane Towne, USA 00000
	[1] September 13 – October 12,2021
Account Number: 001-00011001	[2] 0

Account Summary [3]	
Opening balance 9/14	$88.78
Deposits and other credits [6]	2775.29
Interest paid [5]	0
Checks and debits [7]	2,818.97
Closing balance 10/12 [9]	45.10

Deposits and Other Credits [6]

Date	Amount	Description
13-Sep	$930.65	Your paycheck – Auto Deposit
16-Sep	409.00	Deposit
27-Sep	65.00	Refund – Target 0001 02/19
30-Sep	440.00	Deposit
30-Sep	930.65	Your paycheck – Auto Deposit

Checks and Debits [7]

Date	Amount	Description
16-Sep	$5.00	YMCA Dues – Draft [11]
17-Sep	1.00	Charge for ATM debit [12]
17-Sep	20.00	ATM withdrawal [10]
7-Oct	1.00	Charge for ATM debit [12]
7-Oct	20.00	ATM withdrawal [10]
10-Oct	9.00	Maintenance Fee [4]

Checks [7]

Date	Number	Amount	Date	Number	Amount
23-Aug	7520*	$5.00	23-Sep	7666	$23.40
16-Sep	7663	48.21	24-Sep	7667	13.44
17-Sep	7664	54.82	26-Sep	7668	20.34
27-Sep	7665	26.62	1-Oct	7669	28.04

* Indicates a break in check number sequences

Daily Balances [8]

Date	Balances	Date	Balances
9-13	$1,019.43	9-26	$474.15
9-16	1,309.64	9-27	529.35
9-17	976.32	9-30	948.63
9-24	714.32	10-7	54.10
9-25	73.13	10-10	[9] 45.10

The First Step

You can either organize your cancelled checks in numerical order (I don't bother), or you can begin now.

> ☞ Not all banks return checks. Your checks may be listed in numerical order on your statement, or they may appear on an additional page as photocopies of the original check.

1. Look at the first check.
2. Find the check number in your checkbook register.

> ☞ If your bank statement lists the checks on your statement instead of providing the cancelled checks or photocopies, you won't be able to compare the payee name or date, only the check number and amount.

You should be able to view the front and back of the check online.

> ☞ If you find a mistake in the amount, it's okay. Make a note of the check number and whether the difference is greater or less than what you recorded in your check register. You will record this amount as a correction in your check register later.

> ☞ Be sure to use a calculator for an accurate figure.

3. Compare the amount, date, and payee name to what you entered in the check register.

4. If everything is correct, place a check mark in the column as shown below.

CK # / Debit	DATE	DESCRIPTION OF TRANSACTION	PAYMENT/ DEBIT (-)		✓	DATE	DEPOSIT / CREDIT (+)		BALANCE 402.27	
2501	4-12	Don's Repair Shop	18	98	✓				383	29

5. Repeat this procedure until all checks and debits, such as monthly automatic deductions, are checked off.

6. Repeat this procedure for all deposit transactions.

7. Next, repeat this procedure for all automatic teller (ATM/Banking Card) withdrawals.

8. Now, go to the end of your checkbook register to the last entry. Enter any service charges and deduct them from the ending checkbook balance.

> Highlight any transactions on your bank statement that were not included in your check register.

These unlisted transactions will have to be entered and deducted/added later.

> When you check off every item on a check register page, place an "X" through the page, from corner to corner.

The next time you balance your checkbook, you know that everything on that page has been processed and it will save you from having to look through those transactions.

CK # / Debit	DATE	DESCRIPTION OF TRANSACTION	PAYMENT/ DEBIT (-)		✓	DATE	DEPOSIT / CREDIT (+)		BALANCE 402.27	
2501	4-12	Don's Repair Shop	18	98	✓				383	29
2502	4-12	Herbie's Health Food	27	36	✓	6-11	1107	32	355	93
2503	4-13	Auto Fix-It Place Oil Change	12	95	✓				342	98
2504	4-15	Grabb Insurance Co.	9	50	✓				333	48
2505	4-17	YMCA Weight Class	10	50	✓				322	98
ATM	4-20	Money for kids	20	00	✓				302	98

9. Add any interest payment if your account is an interest-bearing account.

10. Record any missing transactions or corrections you noted. Deduct these from your ending checkbook balance.

You are finished with the first part of this process.

Take a breather.

You survived.

Bringing Up the Rear

This section is like a reconnaissance mission. You are going to search for outstanding debits and credits... otherwise known as checks and transactions that have not been processed yet.

1. Turn on and clear your calculator to zero.
2. Start at the beginning of your checkbook register and look for pages you have not made an X through. These pages contain outstanding transactions.

3. Each time you come to a check, ATM/Banking Card deduction, or automated payment that has not been checked off, enter the amount in the calculator.
4. When you have completed that task, write the figure on the **right-hand side** of a piece of paper or the back of your bank statement.
5. **Label this checks outstanding.**
6. Underneath this figure, write your checkbook balance and label this **checkbook balance**.
7. Add the two figures together.
8. Next, clear the calculator back to zero, then return to your checkbook register. Look for any deposits not included in your statement.
9. Add them together and write this figure on the **left-hand side** of your paper, labeling these **deposits outstanding**.
10. Underneath this figure, write your **bank statement balance**.

> Make sure you use the balance from your most current bank statement.

11. Add these figures together.

12. Compare the two final figures.

I CALL the right-hand side **MY SIDE** and the left-hand side the **BANK'S SIDE.**

Bank's Side		My Side	
$1198.13	Bank Statement Balance	$546.35	Checks Outstanding
+ 230.00	Deposits Outstanding	+ 884.78	Checkbook Balance
$1428.13		$1428.13	

If the figures are identical, you are balanced! Throw a party! You did it all by yourself and saved yourself a bundle of money.

Why pay someone to perform this service when you can balance your own checkbook yourself and see exactly where your money goes each month?

Had you brought all of your statements to the bank for the customer service department to do it, they could have charged you approximately $15-$25 per hour.

Those figures weren't twins? Use the calculator and subtract to see what the difference is.

Bank's Side		My Side	
$1198.13	Bank Statement Balance	$546.35	Checks Outstanding
+ 230.00	Deposits Outstanding	+ 79.87	Checkbook Balance
$1428.13		$1423.22	

$4.91 difference. OOPS!!

If the bank has more than you do, that's great. If your side has more than the bank, that's not so great.

You have two options for this unmatched balance:

1. Adjust your checkbook balance, or
2. Begin at the beginning of your checkbook register and

rework your math, adding and subtracting until you find your mistake.

	Be sure to examine your checks to make sure you entered the correct amount in your check register.

If you choose Step 1, you will **subtract** from your checkbook balance if **your side** has more money.

Add if the **bank's side** has more.

Why? Because you probably made a mistake in your math.

Banks aren't perfect either, but you have to balance to the tune of the amount on the statement.

Place a check mark in the check mark column after you complete this step.

	If your discrepancy is less than one dollar, adjust your balance. However, if the amount is significant on your side and you cannot find the error by reworking your check register(s), call your bank and make an appointment with the customer service department. You may even want to request an audit.

If you have not balanced your account for many months and don't think you can manage tackling it now, open a new account.

Leave your old account alone for at least 60 days until all checks are processed. Then close the account. Good riddance! Shred all unused checks.

> Never throw away unused checks unless they are marred to make them unusable. Crooks love to find bundles of checks!

10

STARTING OVER

Now that you are starting fresh, either with a new account or a balanced account, it is time to change your habits and thinking regarding your money transactions.

Your checkbook can be your financial guru telling you where every cent is spent, thereby making it easier for you to keep track of where your salary goes.

You may even find it easier keeping tabs on deductible items for income tax purposes.

Never rely on your memory to document something at a later date.

Take the time to record the transaction at the time of the transaction. It only takes a second and in the long run, it will save you an overdraft slip.

> When you balance your checking account monthly, it is easier to prevent fraud. An unbalanced account may have suspicious transactions that could lead to someone stealing your money or your identity.

What This is All About

Think of this process as learning a new method of becoming financially solvent.

1. Look at your checkbook balance.
2. Determine any expenses coming up between now and your next paycheck.
3. If you can afford it, take $100 and deduct it from your balance.
4. Place the date in the date column and write **save for checkbook** in the description of transaction column. If that figure is out of the ballpark, any figure will do, even $5.00.
5. Place a check mark in the column for processed checks, then deduct the amount from your checkbook balance.

> If you can allocate money for partying, cigarettes, or shopping, then you DO have extra cash to set aside.

CK # / Debit	DATE	DESCRIPTION OF TRANSACTION	PAYMENT/ DEBIT (-)		✓	DATE	DEPOSIT / CREDIT (+)		BALANCE 402.27	
2501	4-12	Don's Repair Shop	18	98	✓				383	29
	4-13	Save for Checkbook	100	00	✓				283	29

Repeat this process every time you have the extra money.

Each time you enter a **saved** transaction, bring the balance forward, as shown in the next example, and place a check mark in the processed column.

CK # / Debit	DATE	DESCRIPTION OF TRANSACTION	PAYMENT/ DEBIT (-)		✓	DATE	DEPOSIT / CREDIT (+)		BALANCE 504.22	
	5-1	Save for Checkbook	25	00	✓				479	22
		Balance forward $125								

Build a small nest egg.

If you never have extra cash, try to borrow from someone close to you and explain why you need it.

You must understand at this point that this **saved** money is going to save you a lot of money because you won't have bounced check charges coming at you from all sides.

When you receive money for overtime, refunds, birthdays—whatever the occasion, take a little and put it in your checkbook **saved** account.

Determine what figure will see you through lean times and make that your goal.

Don't forget, you don't have to stop there. You can keep adding to your checkbook **saved** account for when you want to go on a spending spree.

The money will be there if you put it there.

To balance your account when the statement arrives, follow the steps outlined previously to balance your checkbook.

Now, **add** the **saved** amount to **your side** (outstanding checks + checkbook balance + **saved**).

Bank's Side		My Side	
$ 450.44	Bank Statement Balance	$ 487.32	Checks Outstanding
+ 266.00	Deposits Outstanding	104.12	Checkbook Balance
$ 716.44		+ 125.00	Saved for Checkbook
		$ 716.44	

When you need to use your **saved** money, write the dollar amount you are withdrawing in the deposit column, and write **saved** underneath the figure.

Bring your **saved balance** forward every time so you will know exactly what you have in reserve. Place a check mark in the processed column.

CK # / Debit	DATE	DESCRIPTION OF TRANSACTION	PAYMENT/ DEBIT (-)		✓	DATE	DEPOSIT / CREDIT (+)		BALANCE 504.22	
	5-1	Save for Checkbook	25	00	✓				479	22
		Balance forward $125								
2680	5-10	Auto Fix-It	184	13					295	09
2681	5-13	Dr. Dingbat	156	00					139	09
		Sinus infection								
2682	5-14	Yumme Grocery	87	52					51	57
2683	5-15	Internet	44	87					6	70
		From Saved			✓		100	00	106	70
		Saved Balance $25			✓				106	70

Who, What, When and Where

Record-keeping is important. Each time you write a check, make a note.

If you are going to do all of your banking online, you still need a checkbook register to keep your balance, bill payments and automatic deductions current. You can order checkbook registers (for a fee) from an online service such as Checks in the Mail.

Checkbook registers are inexpensive and the best tool you can use. If you don't want to purchase them, create a spreadsheet checkbook register.

- Paying for magazines? Write the names of the magazines under the payee's name in your checkbook register.
- Sending away for something? Write the address under the payee's name; you may need it later.
- Writing a check for car repairs? Document what the check is for. You may forget when you had your last oil change or lose the receipt, but your checkbook register never lies.
- Document where the money comes from—paycheck, gift, refund, etc.

Every time you use your debit card write the transaction in your checkbook register, along with the date.

CK # / Debit	DATE	DESCRIPTION OF TRANSACTION	PAYMENT/ DEBIT (-)		✓	DATE	DEPOSIT / CREDIT (+)		BALANCE 302.98	
2690	6-1	Bob's Lawn Service	80	00					222	98
		Trim trees & shrubs								
2691	6-10	Animal Clinic	30	00		6-11	1107	32	1300	30
		Heart worm medicine					Tax Refund			
2692	6-13	Lee's Liquor	12	82					1287	48
		Party								
Debit	6-14	Gas Station	35	98					1251	50
		OD 12,334								

Do not rely on your memory. Your memory is the enemy!

Ask your bank if they charge a fee for each ATM transaction at your bank and/or other ATM locations.

Additional service charges may apply and be deducted automatically every time you use your ATM/banking card.

When you write a check for a tax-deductible item, highlight the item with a marker. You'll thank yourself later. Also consider starting a separate document, perhaps in Excel, for tax deductions.

No one can remember everything they purchased during an entire year, but you can make your checkbook register work for you by keeping track of all important transactions.

11

BEWARE, POTENTIAL DANGERS LURK OUT THERE

Save your deposit slips until you balance your bank statement. If you deposit **cash** and do not keep the receipt, you could set yourself up for a disaster.

It doesn't make any difference if you know the teller's name, the date and time you deposited the money, or the serial numbers on the bills. The only saving grace you will have in case the deposit is not posted to your account is that little slip of paper that proves the deposit actually took place.

Properly recording automatic teller (ATM/banking/debit card) transactions is a MUST. How many times have you gone to one of those priceless machines, inserted your card, and the thing didn't work?

If you record all your transactions, you will catch one or two snafus from those instances when the machine took your card, recorded the number, but didn't give you a dime.

Major Danger

A top military man? No, it's YOU when you call the bank, go online, or check your balance at an ATM.

That's not your REAL balance.

That figure is the balance at that instance from the last time the bank posted transactions in your account.

You have no way of knowing how many of the checks you wrote in the past month have been processed unless you download your bank statement or call your bank's 24-hour banking line to find out which of your last transactions have cleared.

You may have several checks outstanding, a forgotten online bill-payment may process, or an automatic payment may post.

This is one reason you should balance your checkbook every month and the reason you should keep a running balance in your checkbook register every single day.

Otherwise, how are you going to know how much money you have in your account?

How can you tell when it is safe to write a check or use your debit card? You can't guess at these things... you need to be accurate.

Go online frequently to print out transactions, or call your bank's 24-hour banking line to keep your checkbook register up-to-date.

Last but not least, save your bank statements and filled checkbook registers. Do not throw them away.

File them in a box and put them in a closet or the attic; you may need them to substantiate a purchase or a tax deduction.

12

FOR PRACTICE

Maintaining Your Checkbook Register

Enter the following list into the practice blank checkbook register page.

Make sure you place each item in the correct position in the register.

Do the math to show your correct balance when all the transactions are entered into the checkbook register.

> Look at the examples in this booklet for the proper placement of transactions.

- Check 1236, June 12, $102.56, Dog Care Clinic, Raspberry's yearly shots
- Deposit - June 12, $400.00, IRS refund
- Save for checkbook - June 12, $100, balance forward $110

- ATM withdrawal - June 13, $20
- Check 1237, June 13, $87.36, Walmart, battery for Honda
- ATM withdrawal - June 15, $100, vacation
- Debit card - June 15, $32.55, Exxon, gas, vacation
- ATM withdrawal - June 20, $60 + $1.50 ATM charge, vacation

Sample Blank Checkbook Register

CK # / Debit	DATE	DESCRIPTION OF TRANSACTION	PAYMENT/ DEBIT (-)		✓	DATE	DEPOSIT / CREDIT (+)		BALANCE	
			Fold line / staples							

13

FILLING OUT A BLANK CHECK

You have just opened your first checking account, and you only have blank temporary checks.

Using the information below, fill in the sample check.

- Enter your name, address and phone number
- Enter a check number
- Write the date
- Make the check payable to Delray's Auto Center for $212.65 for tires on the Chevy
- Sign the check

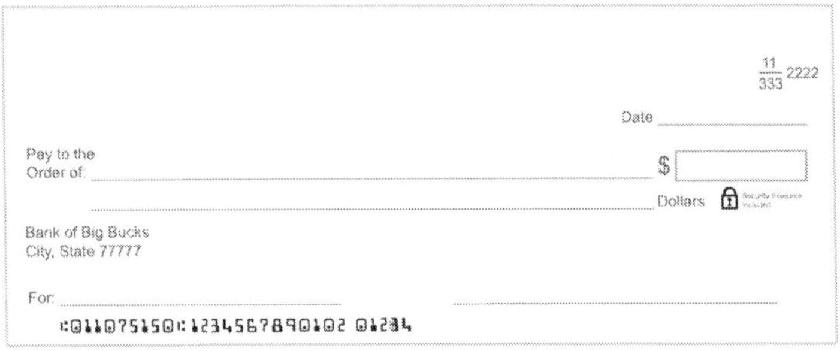
11/333 2222

Date

Pay to the
Order of: $

Dollars

Bank of Big Bucks
City, State 77777

For:

14

COMPLETED EXAMPLES

Sample Check

1002

Mary Gooberstein
5344 Helloway Rd.
Towne, TX 77755
222-777-4444

11/333 2222

Date July 20, 2021

Pay to the Order of: Delray's Auto Center $ 212.65

Two Hundred Twelve & 65/00 Dollars

Bank of Big Bucks
City, State 77777

For: Tire for the Chevy

Mary Gooberstein

011075150 1234567890102 01234

Sample Checkbook Register

CK # / Debit	DATE	DESCRIPTION OF TRANSACTION	PAYMENT/ DEBIT (-)		✓	DATE	DEPOSIT / CREDIT (+)		BALANCE 402.27	
1236	6-12	Dog Care Clinic	102	56					299	71
		Raspberry's shot								
	6-12	IRS Refund					400	00	699	71
	6-12	Save for Checkbook	100	00	✓				599	71
ATM	6-13	ATM Withdrawal	20	00					579	71
1237	6-13	Walmart	87	36					492	35
		Battery for Honda								
ATM	6-15	ATM Withdrawal	100	00					392	35
		Beach								
Debit	6-15	Phil's Gas Emporium	32	55					359	80
		Gas/Beach								
ATM	6-20	ATM Withdrawal	60	00					299	80
		ATM charge/fee	1	50					298	30

BLANK BUDGET TO DOWNLOAD

Cut and paste this blank budget to your computer to use.

My Budget

Payment Method*	Who Pays?**	Monthly Expense/Bill	Due Date	Amount $***
		TOTAL per month		$

*CK – check, Auto – automatic deduction, D – debit card, CC – credit card,
OL – online bill pay, CA – cash.

** Me (I pay), Creditor pays

*** Rounded up to the next dollar.

Take home pay: $

Budget: $

Left over: $

FEEDBACK

I hope you benefited from the information in this booklet.

If you have comments or questions, or **if you would like a licensing agreement to share this booklet with your employees, group, or students,** send me an email.

Consider reading *What's Breaking Your Budget* to continue your education on personal finance.

dawn@dawngreenfieldireland.com

www.dawngreenfieldireland.com/living-smart

ABOUT THE AUTHOR

Dawn Greenfield Ireland is an award-winning technical and creative writer with extensive experience researching, organizing and scheduling projects.

She has been a technical writer since pencils were invented. Now she spends her time writing novels and nonfiction books, and creating online classes. Dawn edits, formats and publishes books. Need a writing coach to finish your project? Give her a holler.

Checkout the online classes, novels and other books.

The correct practice answer is $298.30.

Connect with me on Social Media:

www.smashwords.com/books/view/1118119

www.amazon.com/author/dawnireland

www.Facebook.com/dawn.ireland.18

www.Twitter.com/dawnireland

www.Instagram.com/DawnGreenfieldIreland

goodreads.com/dawnireland

linkedin.com/dawnireland

Made in United States
Orlando, FL
04 November 2026

90203672R00055